BREAKING BARRIERS WITH HYPNOTHERAPY

Digital transformation expressly demands personal transformation. To become digital means to be even more human

MICHAELA ESSWEIN

DEDICATION

This book is specially dedicated to all humans who inspired my interest and awareness towards human potentials, growth, and development. All motivated and encouraged me to venture into this great adventure that has turned out to be quite great and wonderful.

WHY YOU NEED THIS BOOK

Hypnosis and Hypnotherapy emphasizes the importance of working with a hypnotherapist to achieve your goals. Developing a working relationship with your hypnotherapist is the key to achieving a positive outcome. I think that this is a significant difference to many introductory books on hypnotherapy. Many of those currently available falls into two main types:

- **Specific interest books**

Aimed at anyone interested in solving a particular problem. These books focus on a single issue, such as the application of hypnosis to achieve weight control, decrease anxiety, develop confidence, or to stop smoking, and so on.

- **Scripts books**

Aimed at teaching a DIY (do-it-yourself) approach to hypnosis. Scripts are the phrases hypnotherapists use to conduct therapy, once someone is in trance. These types of books offer techniques you can use to hypnotize yourself or others.

In my opinion, this DIY approach cannot approach the level of trance or range of techniques that a good hypnotherapist can provide. I have seen many clients in my years of practice who have had zero, or negative results, from amateur hypnosis learned from books alone. A qualified hypnotherapist has a variety of techniques to choose from, and selects the technique uniquely suited to relieving your symptom efficiently and effectively.

I think you need this book, because unlike specific interest books, this book takes a broad overview of the theory and practice of hypnosis and hypnotherapy, examining a wide range of the most common hypnotherapy treatments.

TABLE OF CONTENTS

Dedication .... *iii*
Why You Need This Book .... *v*

Introduction 1

Chapter 1: Understanding What Hypnosis Is 3
    What is hypnosis? 3
    Who Is A Hypnotist? 7
    Misconceptions About Hypnosis 7
    The Facts You Should Know About Hypnosis 10

Chapter 2: The History Of Hypnosis 21

Chapter 3: Understanding Hypnotherapy And What It Can Help Achieve 35
    Understanding The Differences Between Hypnosis and Hypnotherapy 37
    Stage Hypnosis Is Not Hypnotherapy 38
    Going into Trance 39
    Finding Help With Hypnotherapy 41
    Understanding the Therapeutic Part of Hypnotherapy 42
    Going To Your First Hypnotherapy Session 43

Chapter 1: Conscious, Subconscious And Superconscious 53
    The Conscious Mind 54

The Subconscious Mind 55
The Superconscious Mind 56
The Age Long Battle Between Willpower And Imagination 57
When Will Power And Imagination Clash, The Imagination Often Always Wins 57
The Power of Thought 58
The Universe is Made of Thought 58

Chapter 4: The Power Of Suggestion 61

A Three Step Learning Pattern 62
Suggestibility vs Gullibility 62
How People Respond To Suggestions 63
Taking Responsibility 65
Your Inner Lie Detector 65
Beliefs 67
Selective Thinking 68
The Best Way To Deliver Suggestions 68
Pre-Hypnotic Suggestion (The Pretalk) 71
Being in the Moment 71
Post-Hypnotic Analysis 72
Compounding Suggestions 73
Post Hypnotic Suggestion 75
Waking Suggestion 75
Waking Trance 77
Rejecting Suggestions 78
Great Ways to Program or Reprogram Your Subconscious 79

Chapter 5: Formulating Positive Suggestions 81
    How To Develop Effective Suggestions 83
    How to Edit Your Affirmations 85
    Post Hypnotic Suggestions 87

Chapter 6: The Things That Influence Your Ability To Respond 89
    Three Important things necessary for Hypnosis to occur 90
    Mental Expectancy 91
    Ambiance 92

Chapter 7: Understand That Hypnotherapy Has Its Limitations 95
    You Must Learn To Accept The Limitations Of Hypnotherapy 97
    Your Symptom 97
    Your Expectations 98
    Your Fears 98
    Your Relationship With The Hypnotherapist 99

INTRODUCTION

Hypnosis is a subject matter that almost everyone has an opinion about but quite few persons have had a firsthand experience. Hypnosis is arguably one of the oldest forms of Western Psychology and Avicama, a Persian physician first documented the hypnotic state in the year 1027. After years of misrepresentations and misconceptions, it is heartwarming and sweet to see that hypnosis is fast regaining its credibility. When you watch movies and TV shows, those guys always present hypnosis in a stereotypical line that goes "you are getting sleepy, very sleepy". What nonsense; that is not even close to what hypnosis is. Well, thank goodness I have this book that will reposition your mind on the beauty and loveliness of hypnosis. In some of these movies, you must have seen scenes where hypnosis has been depicted as "magic." You must have seen a patient or volunteer stares at a ball swinging and in minutes turn into a zombie that is highly susceptible to the hypnotists every whim. Seeing such things must have left you wondering and cracking your brains out about the meaning of hypnosis. Please crack your brains no more so you don't come down with headache. I will help you to understand what hypnosis means and how it is different from hypnotherapy. Yea, you heard me; hypnosis is quite different from hypnotherapy and I am going to explain all to you in this informative and highly educative book. So, you grab a cup of tea or wine because you are going to be glued to this book for quite a long while and trust me you wouldn't want to be doing that without a form of refreshment. You will discover from this book that the natural powers of your own mind can serve you and the world around you your very best capacities through the basic skills of hypnosis. Don't be surprised to find that these methods are familiar to you as you already use them every day, even if you are not consciously paying attention. I welcome you specially to the study of how to relax fully, engage the indwelling spark of creativity that resides inside you.

CHAPTER ONE

UNDERSTANDING WHAT HYPNOSIS IS

To help you understand what hypnosis is and what it entails, let me define hypnosis in a very simple and first grade terms. I do hope you are not angry am going to define this term as a first grader.

WHAT IS HYPNOSIS?

You should see hypnosis as a form of relaxation technique in which you follow specific steps to attain a state of heightened concentration and relaxations. This is referred to as the "hypnotic state." It is also similar to daydreaming or that beautiful feeling of losing track of the time eg- when you are in love, passionate in your job or have a healthy and wonderful sexuality, in these cases you are quite relaxed and at peace with your environment. The word "hypnosis" comes from the Greek word for sleep, "Hypnos". The hypnosis you will be learning in this book is not the sleep - you sleep at night. Hypnosis is more like a sleep from the outside, the subjective experience is often one of heightened awareness. Only a very small percentage of people who practice hypnosis report having no conscious memory of the experience after it have been complete. More common are the individual's report of feelings of well-being after the session of hypnosis.

The hypnotic experience is familiar to anyone who has gotten a greater sense of being such as that which one experiences when functioning smoothly as part of a team, during a peak athletic or creative performance, during moments of break-through creativity and excellence in performance, and when comprehending a sense of connection with something greater than oneself within the limits of one's own skin. The theoretical foundation for this book is spiritual monism; all things are assumed to be coming from the creatively thinking stuff of which the universe is made, call it whatever you like.

Hypnosis is a familiar state and is often encountered when returning to waking state from sleep (hypnopompic), and when entering sleep (hypnogogic). Some people pass through this state hardly noticing it at all. Some pass through slowly, or deliberately seek it out through meditative, creative, or sporting practices. Hypnosis is a natural state which you have been in many situations. Perhaps you can recall a time when you were on the freeway, driving past a familiar exit, your exit, or perhaps you suddenly became aware of yourself behind the wheel as you respond to something that startles you while driving. The thought may have floated through your mind that you hadn't been paying attention to the road for a lengthy period of time. Your attention and conscious mind became absorbed in something other than what your body was doing at that moment, because that part of you that had learned to do certain actions automatically, such as driving, took over. Your automatic functioning continues until something out of the ordinary or dangerous occurs that awakens your consciousness.

You may choose this eBook to no more about hypnosis and how it will help you. As you gong regularly to hypnosis, you may find yourself becoming more and more aware of your capacity to respond to suggestion. Your continued reading reflects your growing curiosity about the possibilities that are inherent within you. This learning is best done experientially, subjectively, so as to gain familiarity and fluidity with the natural human capacity for relaxation. Trust yourself. You are going to learn how to recognize the signs of hypnosis, how to go to a Hypnosis-therapist, and how to recognize the preferred responses you can expect to encounter. Some people will be slower or more difficult than others. Some will move so quickly they will steam roll you to move faster or get out of their way.

The reputation of the word hypnosis evokes images of strange and mysterious powers and people, faith healers and sideshows, yet the human response to suggestion is as natural as the sky's response of light with the approach of dawn. Hypnosis has such a rich and powerful history of creating change and this has made Hollywood to use it to embellish movie scenes. The human mind is amazing, and you will learn to identify and debunk the Hollywood hype and common misconceptions that distort the usefulness of this natural human function once you are done reading this book.

For the purposes of this book, the term hypnosis will be used to define any technique which promotes direct and/or automatic communication between that which you are consciously aware of, and the subconscious, emotional, imaginative mind, the warehouse of your learning and knowledge. Inside you lies a being that knows everything about you, and it knows that it knows. This being knows what you like, dislike, and want or need that you haven't gotten, yet. Hypnosis is a tool that, when used correctly, can bring astonishing and often rapid results through simply learning to relax yourself the right way. Then add the focus of attention upon specific goals, with clarity of intent, present tense, and subjective ownership. Wonders await those who explore the mysteries of the mind through the use of hypnosis.

WHO IS A HYPNOTIST?

Misinformation and misconceptions about the nature of suggestion and response leads the public to believe that a hypnotist has some kind of magical power. A Hypnotist is a person trained to give detailed attention to semantics, voice inflection, body movement and generating mental expectancy from an individual. A skilled hypnotist has learned methods for bypassing the critical faculty and establishing selective thinking. The hypnotist's job is to use suggestion to excite the imagination and develop a mental expectancy in the subject or individual. You can observe suggestion in action through the repetition, emotional baiting, direct, implied, and embedded messages of advertising, education, marketing, and politics.

MISCONCEPTIONS ABOUT HYPNOSIS

People have come to associate hypnosis with so many things that are entirely parallel to the actual meaning of hypnosis. Often times, people tend to think that hypnosis is a form of mind control where you will be made to act against your will. This can't be further from the truth as hypnosis is never a form a mind control. You should always remember that. In fact, hypnosis is very similar to meditation where you follow steps that allow you to enter into a state of deep concentration and relaxation. The most important thing to note is that you remain in control throughout this process. It is quite unfortunate that pop culture has completely tarnished the image of hypnosis and pushed forward some silly and ridiculous misconceptions. The common ones include the following:

- **You lose control**

If you haven't heard, then let me be the first to inform you that hypnotized people are totally and completely aware of their environment and surroundings. Such people tune out distractions, reach relaxation, and ultimately calm the mind. You should remember that there is no loss of control as suggests by most movies and TV shows.

- **You are either asleep or unconscious**

This is another huge misconception that the public holds about hypnosis. They often mistake the deep focus and relaxation reached during hypnosis for sleep or unconsciousness. That is exactly why the origin of the word hypnosis is "Hypnos" which translates to sleep in English. The major difference is that unlike sleep or unconsciousness, you are completely aware of all that is happening.

- **You can get stuck in hypnosis**

You can see them in more movies than one, where someone attempts hypnosis for the very first time and he or she never wakes up. What a complete lie and distortion of the truth and fact. In such movies, such individuals often stay hypnotized forever. Always remember that in hypnosis, you can open your eyes anytime you want and come back into your surroundings.

- **Hypnosis is a magic bullet**

Yea, people often say that hypnosis is not a cure. You definitely want to make a difference, and you have to continue to work at it. But if you actually want to improve, research has shown that hypnotherapy can help.

- **The hypnotist has strange and unknown powers**

I believe you also hear that hypnotists like us are magicians and that we possess strange powers. Well, next time someone tells you that you reply them that every human being alive has great power at his or her disposal whether such a person is a hypnotist or a football player. We are endowed with great power. So, no hypnotist has any such magical powers.

Misconceptions about the natural state of hypnosis can elicit a fear response to hypnosis in members of the general public who do not understand the underlying assumptions of what hypnosis is, and what can be done with hypnosis to improve personal performance and relaxation restoration experiences. Keeping the general public in a state of fear regarding hypnosis, Hollywood hype and unscrupulous operators can use the public's lack of information to make a buck. It is to tackle such misconceptions that I have written this book to educate my clients. I always make it a point of duty to identify my client's misconceptions and debunk it out rightly before we start any session. I debunk the myths of hypnosis and establish a collaborative relationship.

THE FACTS YOU SHOULD KNOW ABOUT HYPNOSIS

- **All hypnosis is self hypnosis**

A hypnotist is a helper or assistant with a set of tools or skills that humans have found to be useful in creative rapid transformation in human growth and development. The expertise of a humanistically oriented hypnotherapist is in skill development so as to have a broad range of approaches to offer a hypnotic subject. The subject being hypnotized is using the hypnotist as a helpful assistant with a broad range of tools to offer for ease of entering and exiting the relaxed state known as hypnosis. The client is the expert in self. The state of hypnosis is natural. It is only a matter of recognition, and then skill development for use of the state for a range of experiences from deep relaxation and restoration of self, to peak performance and creativity flow.

In hypnosis, the subject becomes much more aware of his or her perceptions than full waking state. Rather than restricting the senses, hypnosis expands and magnifies the senses, with particularly enhanced selectivity for the focus of attention. A hypnotic subject cannot be made to do or say anything that might be damaging to the self. Inside each individual is a knowing that knows everything about that person and knows that it knows. At some level, the individual is always aware and in control. He or she can choose to accept or reject any idea or suggestion that is determined to be unacceptable. A hypnotized person cannot be made to do anything against his or her personal, moral or religious beliefs. The subject won't tell any secrets he or she doesn't want known. People in hypnosis laugh, cry, move, open and close their eyes, talk, think and feel just like people in full waking state. The subject is always aware at some level, and must be able to hear for the suggestions to work, must be able to see in the mind's eye, hear with the inner ear, and perceive with an inner knowing. Although the hypnotic methods focused on in this manual involve the use of relaxation, the experience of hypnosis is not limited to relaxation. Hypnosis is also recognizable in states of heightened activity, arousal, physical activity, being in the zone of one's peak performance. The only time someone fails to emerge into full waking state when requested to return by the hypnotist, is when the individual is enjoying the relaxation so much that a return to the stresses and strains of daily life is postponed, voluntarily, by that subject. You can't get stuck in hypnosis any more than you can get stuck in sleep.

In hypnosis, the critical faculty of the mind is bypassed and the imaginative faculty is engaged. The critical faculty is the judge and censor of the conscious mind. When it is bypassed, selective thinking to help improve performance and overcome blockages can be established. The subject will bypass the critical faculty when there is a sufficient level of self trust and other trust developed between the hypnotist and the subject. The sufficient level of trust is known as rapport. As you learn to establish better rapport with yourself and others, you will find it easier and easier to explore deep, profound relaxation. Through this relaxation, a more direct communication or communion with your inner wisdom is reestablished. The ability to self regulate oneself with a relaxed feeling of well being allows for the hypnotist to establish and maintain a safe, bounded and unbounded environment within which the process of growth with its unfolding development expands in ways that transcend the wisdom of the members physically present. Rapport can come about through direct suggestion, waking suggestion, or any of the innumerable natural occurrences which you may have heard referred to as hypnosis, trance, meditation, prayer, relaxation, bliss, rapport, contentment, well being, empathy, compassion, peak performance and epiphany.

You are already familiar with hypnosis because it occurs naturally when you are under stress, thinking deeply, half asleep and half awake, driving, reading . . . anytime the deep creative resources of the inner mind are called forth. You are particularly sensitive to suggestion and response in times of repetition, intense emotions, powerful longing and feelings of identification.

In hypnosis, you know everything going on and you know that you know. You know what you are saying, hearing, doing. Your perception capacities become enhanced, as does your ability to focus, or defocus. The sounds of the world around you become background sounds that reassure you all is well in the outside world. You are safe to go deeper into hypnosis. Imagine that the sky is blue, and all things float away like a little puffy cloud on a beautiful day. Should anything occur which requires your immediate attention; you are immediately alert and ready to respond with full capacity. For now, just float, drift, relax. Become aware.

While practicing hypnosis you can speak, move, laugh, cry, blink, or yawn because you are always in control. Just like any form of exercise, every time you practice self hypnosis, you achieve better response. The more you relax, the deeper you go, the deeper you go, the more relaxed you will be. The better the response the deeper you go into your own knowing.

Each and every time easier, deeper, faster and better than the times before and it calls you and you listen, listen, listen, and deep inside there is wisdom. I'm talking to you now. And you are curious. Perhaps, so curious and that is the feeling that I am talking about.

Once you have recognized the many times you have already used self hypnosis successfully (and automatically) in the past, you can learn how to use it consciously for greater self awareness, satisfaction, and relaxation. The reason you don't recognize the state of hypnosis is because you generally don't discuss it with people. It is a natural state that you take for granted like your heartbeat! Unless you've had a heart disorder, it is a rare topic of conversation to say, "Yes, my heart is beating today. All your life, you have been hypnotizing yourself without a formal language to describe what you are doing. You hypnotize yourself on a daily basis. You learned through empathic mirroring engaging with other humans, and you learned to automatically and hypnotically state regulation through repetitive practice.

You go in and out of the relaxed state of hypnosis automatically when you drive, read, run up a flight of stairs, zip a zipper. All automatically. You just haven't been formally trained to recognize it the way you were trained to know the alphabet, word identification, and the sentence structure of written or spoken material such as this. As you read or listen to these words, you are using reading or listening trance. You understand what words are meant to symbolize through repetitive practice. You learned to read by focusing your attention on letters, words and sentences until the process became automatic. You observed, perceived sounds, body language, intonation, pace, and behavior until you mastered the art of communication in the family, cultural, and temporal context within which you were raised. It is only a lack of formal training that causes you to fail to consciously identify or acknowledge the natural method by which you get your MENTAL POWER to work for you. Most people take this natural state for granted. If you pay attention, you may find that you rarely stop to think about how you do what you do, and why you do all the things you do, when you do them. You just do them. The things you do automatically are done because you have, at some point in time, trained yourself to do them. When you pay attention, it is called mindfulness or awareness of self. You didn't leap from your mother's womb into reading, cooking, or driving. You taught yourself numerous steps so well, that you are now able to do some things automatically.

As you learn language skills to describe this simple and much used Mind Power, you automatically reconnect with how you think and feel which may be different from what other people say you are supposed to think or feel. What is life really all about when you think and feel, using your own perceptions and senses completely. Realign with WHAT IS instead of What If because that is what elicits your metal consciousness. This is the objective of an existential / humanistic approach to hypnosis and hypnotherapy. It is based on the Gestalt concepts of Fritz Perls.

Hypnosis and meditation are similar in the goal of ease, peace of mind and relaxation. The difference between meditation and hypnosis is the purpose or intent. The intent of some forms of meditation is nothingness, Oneness with the all knowing Void. Some meditations seek to be completely in the moment, perceiving with fresh eyes, putting aside preconceived notions so as to trust one's senses and perceptions. The purpose of hypnosis is to relax the conscious mind so that the natural functioning of the subconscious and super conscious are focusing their creative powers on achieving a particular goal or set of goals. Allow yourself to align with the mission that is most dear to your higher purpose, your innermost striving, aligning for the best for all involved. Instead of trying hard and fearing failure or success, you can learn to relax and let the subconscious mind work with, instead of against, your conscious plans. The logical mind can come up with all kinds of reasons and excuses for failing. It will interest you to know that when properly applied, the mind can come up with just as many reasons for success, relaxed enjoyment of living, and peak performance strategies.

All people have an ability to respond to hypnosis and you are equal to any human, living or dead, that ever inhabited this planet. When you want to respond to hypnosis and you are temporarily out of control, you should stop trying. You should allow it happen to the best of your ability at that moment by simply breathing. Pay close attention to the response of your senses, your sensual response should be consciously monitored at all times. What you hear, see, smell, feel, taste, touch, imagine, perceive, and experience matters a lot. You are an air breathing mammal. Hypnosis is subjective and you will experience it in your own unique way. Some things you will have in common with other people who experience hypnosis, some things will be idiosyncratic or unique to you. Sometimes you will notice a certain familiarity or predictability to the type of response you experience, and you may reach plateaus in your capacity and practice with self and others. At other times, you may notice your response to hypnosis change radically, or gradually shifting to something new. Trust yourself; discover the wonder of being a lifelong learner on this amazing subject of human growth and development. When you invest yourself in taking basic hypnosis courses every so often, you will hear familiar information, and will also begin to hear it in ways that you did not recognize or identify when you first started this formal study of hypnosis. Hypnosis is a natural state. All humans can benefit from skills training to be able to articulate and identify hypnotic phenomenon and harness it for its remarkable applications to learning and test taking, creativity, peak performance, preparation for surgery, business and personal relationships, healing, and spiritual development.

The biggest payoff of experiencing hypnosis, and the one thing all people who practice the skills of this course have in common, is a sense of deep, profound relaxation which becomes an automatic reflex with practice. You will practice self regulation for relaxed well being throughout this course, and as you practice you will notice interesting things about yourself, and you are curious. You will find it wonderfully pleasing to regu late your state for a relaxed well being more easily with each repetition of the exercises in this course, and you are curious about how you will first notice the effects of your mind power in relaxing, being, unfolding your innate capacities. If you don't respond completely to suggestions of relaxation, at this time, you are responding only to the situation at that time. That doesn't mean you are a poor subject, it means that the circumstances, or the hypnotist, weren't comfortable to you at that time, for whatever reason. Each practice will allow you to experience a deeper and deeper sense of awareness of self, **ALL HYPNOSIS IS SELF HYPNOSIS** (auto hypnosis) and the responsibility for entering trance lies within the subject, you. It is the hypnotist's job to excite the imagination, implanting the expectation of results.

That which is thought, tends to come to fruition. That which is expected, tends to be achieved. The creative forces of your imagination are set into motion by the power of your thoughts. Self hypnosis is a key that opens the door to the treasure house in your mind, the part that knows everything about you and knows that it knows. Everything you've ever experienced or perceived has been faithfully recorded in your memory banks. You've got a log of what worked and what didn't work. You've developed a lot of resources since some of those experiences were logged in with the attached decisions and emotions. The more involved a person becomes in the process of relaxation the easier the response to suggestion. Even those people who resist the process of relaxation are pleasantly surprised to find that the subconscious has recorded suggestions and is using some or all the suggestions appropriately and effectively.

Each and every time you practice self hypnosis you go deeper and faster than the time before. Each and every breath and blink creates a greater rhythm, a balance with the breathing and the heart, and a wonderful rhythm with all the systems of the body, and mind, and spirit. You may be pleasantly surprised, perhaps delighted, as your life unfolds and you find amazing and wonderful things in every day, even when there are storm clouds and challenges on the horizon or overhead. Things pass, days and nights pass, time passes, we all are mortal, we live most fully in each moment and allow yourself to be aware of the full extent of what it means to be human, to be connected, one with a larger being of humanity.

CHAPTER 2

THE HISTORY OF HYPNOSIS

The processes referred to in this book as hypnosis are as old as mankind, stretching from ancient shamans to the present day faith healers and marketing witches and wizards. The ability to respond to suggestion is what creates human community, support and protection, or rejection and ostracism. Every culture uses some form of hypnosis or trance to facilitate community building, establishing of norms, healing and rehabilitation.

In primitive societies, the shaman or medicine man may go to a place in which the environment offers no distractions. The goal is to be strongly focused. A dark quiet space, someplace isolated, in a forest or a cave may be sought out to facilitate the trance state. Some practitioners use drum beats, chanting, singing, or dancing, aids which may be provided by a shaman's companion or by the shaman him or herself. Rhythmic and/or monotonous sounds are useful tools for inducing and enhancing the trance state in most people. In the concepts of soul loss and retrieval, once the shaman enters the state in which his or her mind becomes strongly focused, he/she may seek out the sick spirit in order to return it to the client. Perhaps there is a battle for the spirit. Perhaps the self is splintered, or burdened by parts and ideas that are not beneficial to oneself, thoughts, ideals and behaviors of other people. Spiritual assistance may be called in from other dimensions to assist in the healing. These primitive processes involve imagination, visualization and often suggestion during which the healer wills the sick person to be healed. The intent of the healer is assumed to be of great value in hypnosis, unlike in scientific experiments wherein all efforts are made to avoid experimenter effect. As a hypnotist, learn to lock your mind around the idea that the suggestion you are delivering is fully followed. Lock your mind around the idea of what it is that you intend or hope to achieve. Clarity of intent is productive for effective hypnotic experiences.

Hypnosis has a cross cultural religious and therapeutic history ranging from the ancient cultures of Rome, Greece, India, and Egypt. Apparently all primitive cultures to modern medical practices include processes which are known to modern cultures as hypnosis. The priests and priestesses of Egyptian sleep temples used suggestion to achieve spontaneous and miraculous cures, modern hypnotists use similar processes. The

Greek temples of Aesculapius used suggestions. The processes of hypnosis are natural processes, things that all humans do and experience as they heal, grow, adapt, learn, and change. These processes transcend cultural, religious, and scientific norms.

With the rise of Christianity, for some branches of religious practice, hypnosis was cast in the light of being something evil. Information about the true nature of hypnosis was held in secret by the ruling classes for religious and political power. The uneducated public was led to believe that someone hypnotized was under the control of the hypnotist, and the hypnotist was in league with the devil, unless those using suggestion to influence the minds of others were affiliated with the established religious and political power structure. Then it is the one way, the only way, the true way! In all good lies, there is a seed of truth. The darkest taint of hypnosis in the modern fundamental Christian perspective is that it creates vulnerability to possession. The use of hypnosis does have the potential for increasing ones awareness of spiritual dimension. It is unlikely that hypnosis would be at cause in an issue of spirit haunting, demonizing, or possession. Hypnosis is a tool for expanding awareness beyond the five senses scientifically attributed to the human body for perceiving and measuring the world. Greater awareness of self can create a capacity to recognize and dislodge thoughts, feelings, and behaviors that are not recognized as one's own. It is not uncommon to integrate the thoughts, behaviors, expressions, and feelings of other people who are important to us, into our own thoughts, behaviors, expressions and feelings. It is a normal, empathic capacity of being human to reflect back to others what we observe about them. From the Freudian perspective, it is also a normal defense mechanism to project onto others those things we fear or dislike about ourselves. The fear based injunction to avoid hypnosis appears to be an attempt to keep humans ignorant of natural process for powerful growth and development. Hypnosis can help humans discover more about their potential for growth and development, including the spiritual realms and the innately personal nature of communing with the Divine.

The rise of modern science also cast a shadow on the phenomena we call hypnosis, seeking to distance the hypnotic experience from its spiritual roots. Hypnosis entered the modern medical world in the 1772 when a French physician, Anton Mesmer (1734-1815), introduced his theory of animal magnetism. Mesmer began his studies to be a priest, transferred his studies to law and finally to medicine. At some point, Mesmer observed a priest stroking the bodies of subjects in need of healing. The subjects would apparently fall into a trance and waken free from their presenting problem. Mesmer theorized that there was some form of fluid or energy passing from the hands of the priest through the body that created the healing.

He thought of it as magnetism and thought it could be influenced by magnets. When he asked the French Royal Academy of Science to investigate his "new" methods of healing, he was snubbed. Mesmers success rate was phenomenal. As his fame grew, he needed methods to handle the large numbers of people who flocked to him. He developed a magnetizing system of having people touch iron rods protruding from a large oak tub filled with iron filings. Later he discovered that people could receive the same benefit from touching him. In response to Mesmer's successes, the King of France authorized 5000 francs be sent to Mesmer as a medical research award. Mesmer sent back the 5000 francs with the message that his work was of such fine quality that he deserved double the average award for excellence in medicine. At the time, Ben Franklin was ambassador to France. The King asked Franklin to lead a team of scientific experts to review Mesmer's work. Mesmer is reported to have refused to meet with the King's investigators. The only instances of mesmerism Franklin observed were patients touching the Mesmer's magnetized tree.

After a short observation, Franklin commented that the patients could only be getting well by their own imaginings, articulating the pulse of psychosomatic medicine years before the term was coined. This was used by Mesmer's colleagues to discount his successes and label him a fraud. Psychotherapy was yet to be developed. Those suffering from psychosomatic illness or character disorders received nothing more than reassurance for treatment.

One of Mesmer's disciples, Marquis de Puysegur, believed that the cosmic fluid described by Mesmer was not magnetic, but electric. He was convinced that it came from all living beings, plants as well as animals. He noticed the strange phenomenon of somnambulism associated with hypnosis, phenomena more commonly found among sleep walkers in deep sleep.

In the 1840's a British surgeon, John Elliotson (1791-1868), performed many operations painlessly using animal magnetism. His colleagues condemned him and asked for his resignation as head of the University of London Hospital. Elliotson refused to give up animal magnetism. Chemical anesthesia hadn't been developed yet and hypnosis was too useful. Another British physician, Dr. Esdaile (1808-1859), observed a demonstration of animal magnetism while on vacation in England. He returned to India and performed over 3,000 operations in a prison hospital using nothing but animal magnetism. When he reported his success to the British Medical Association, he was forced to close his hospital and return to England to face charges of charlatanism. He was accused of being sacrilegious because God meant for man to feel pain. After the Queen of England used the newly discovered chloroform to ease her labor pain, the religious theory of people being meant to feel pain was tossed by the wayside in favor of the less painful modern scientific world with its drugs and anesthesia.

In 1840, the word "hypnosis" was coined by James Braid (1795-1860). Braid stumbled upon the state when, while treating a patient with an eye disorder, another man requiring immediate attention arrived. Braid told his first patient that he would be back to have the patient look into a light before administering eye drops. While Braid was tending to the emergency patient, the first patient decided to get ready for the treatment by staring into the light. According to Elman (1964), since Braid recognized the state, he must have already been a closet mesmerist. Braid suggested that his patient close his eyes and he would discover that they just wouldn't work. The man closed his eyes and they wouldn't open. He then told the patient to change his mind and the eyes would work just fine, which they did. Braid concluded that the state was a nervous sleep, based on the way the subject looked to the hypnotist or onlookers and that the state of being occurred when:

- The subject expected to enter trance
- The mesmerist passed hands over the subject's body, thereby transmitting the animal magnetic fluid, and
- Suggestion was given while using eye fixation

Braid distanced his newly discovered phenomena from mesmerism in a time honored manner, by changing the name, thereby avoiding the stigma of mesmerism and the risk being labeled a charlatan. The form of the phenomena did not change, only the naming process. Spiritual assumptions of Divine Intervention, along with hand passes and energy exchange were rejected as insufficiently objective to be subsumed by the material domain of modern medicine. The subtle energy aspects of hypnosis are what science considers secondary perceptual qualities, relating to sensory perceptions and impressions that an individual finds personally meaningful. Primary perceptual qualities involve the perceptions of things which can be objectively measured. Braid selected a word to describe what the state of being looked like objectively, sleep. He named it hypnosis in honor of Hypnos, the Greek god of sleep. Braid's research in hypnosis was published in many languages before he realized that the state is not sleep. When he tried to rename the phenomena "mono-idealism" in order to more accurately describe the enhanced awareness and focal capacity of the hypnosis experience, but "hypnosis" was already accepted as the common term, and has remained so until the present. Braid's labeling of this state infers the most common misconceptions about hypnotism today, that the hypnotized person won't be able to move, speak, hear, or respond because it'll be like he or she is sleeping, unaware.

In the late 1870s, Dr. Jean Martin Charcot (1825-1893), a neurologist and head of the School of Salpetriere in France, described three states of hypnosis:

- Lethargy, (physical relaxation)
- Catalepsy, (limbs remaining in any position they are placed)
- Somnambulism (able to walk, talk and be anesthetized)

Charcot theorized that only "hysterics" were hypnotizable and he referred to hypnosis as a state of hysteria and abnormal neurology. The young Sigmund Freud (1856 - 1939) was drawn to study Charcot's methods and theory. During the 1880s, two French physicians, Hippolyte Bernheim (1837-1919) and Auguste Ambroise Liebeault (1823-1904), established a joint practice adopting Braid's ideas of induction via suggestion. These two men were the first modern physicians to accurately identify hypnosis as a natural phenomenon. Their work was so successful that physicians from around the world came to study, including Sigmund Freud. Freud was researching the use of hypnosis to unlock repressed memories, and was not a good student of hypnosis because of his mistaken belief that deep trance was needed for hypnotic success. Freud, as with many modern hypnotists, was only able to obtain deep trance with a small percentage of his clients. His colleague, Joseph

Breuer (1842 - 1925), was the leading medical hypnotist of the day. Breuer discovered that symptoms were reduced or disappeared after the subject was able to describe their experience. He developed the concept of using catharsis as a tool for healing, with hypnosis to accelerate the process.

After discussing Breuer's findings with him, Freud put aside hypnosis and developed his theories of psychoanalysis. He took a position that humans have both conscious and unconscious processes. Using an iceberg or island as the model, the observed portion above the water represents conscious processes; the submerged portion represents unconscious processes. Carl Jung (1875-1961) added a collective unconscious to Freud's concepts of depth psychology and the structure of personality. Phineas Quimby, a European mesmerist, toured the United States working with people suffering from all types of illnesses. One woman he helped, Mary Morse (nee Baker) Eddie (1821-1910), studied with him and went on to found the Christian Science Church. Mary Baker Eddie refused to use the word hypnosis or mention it as part of the foundation for her teachings; she renamed this familiar process the Science of the Mind. Her teachings incorporated awareness of the positive and negative effect of belief on the mind.

In 1901, a man named Edgar Cayce discovered he could diagnose illnesses and treatments while in trance. Edgar Cayce, the Sleeping Prophet, would give detailed diagnosis of clients' problems without ever meeting some of them in person. Cayce's capacities point to the transpersonal or non-local aspects of mind and being. Cayce died in 1945, but his large library of material which he obtained remotely during trance are available for research at the Association for Research and Enlightenment (A.R.E.) in Virginia Beach.

After WWI, there was a limited, renewed interest in hypnosis, as it offered short cuts in treating battle fatigue, now know as post traumatic stress disorder (PTSD). In general, hypnosis went into a decline during the early 20th century, but was kept alive by entertainers and psychologists.

In 1908, an eight year old boy named Dave Elman became interested in hypnosis. His father was dying of cancer, and a stage hypnotist helped Dave's father live pain free for the last weeks of his life. Elman was inspired. He read everything he could find about hypnosis. Everything he read indicated that a successful hypnotic induction might take anywhere from several minutes to several hours, and required a bright light or other fixation device. While practicing, Elman noticed boredom and eye fatigue. He learned from an eye doctor how to obtain eye fatigue more rapidly, and developed methods of hypnotic induction that reduced the induction time tremendously. Methods such as the Elman Two Finger Technique made hypnosis a more viable tool for medical use. Elman concluded that the subject was always in complete control, able to suspend disbelief from what he called the critical faculty or critical factor of the mind, and able to receive pleasing suggestions. He noted that when improper suggestions were was given, one of two things happened: the subject would reject the suggestion, and/or terminate trance.

Elman proved that there was no one way to hypnotize people properly, because once you learn the elements of suggestion, there are limitless techniques available. He knew it can relieve chronic pain, and can be induced instantly. He went on to teach thousands of physicians his rapid, effective techniques, including the Mayo brothers. At that time, death by anesthesia was a major threat in surgical procedures. The Mayo clinic was able to reduce the amount of anesthesia given through the use of hypnosis by their nurse anesthetists, reducing their rates of death from anesthesia. After WWII, hypnosis experienced another surge of interest, because of the rapid relief it could help provide for those suffering from neuroses brought on by battle.

There were only a couple hundred people in the United State using hypnosis in 1945. By 1955, the British Medical Association reported that hypnosis was a valuable tool in medical treatment. It urged that hypnosis be taught in medical schools, and finally gave a nod of approval for physicians to openly learn and practice hypnosis. In 1958, hypnosis was given approval as a medical modality by the American Medical Association.

In 1975, the title Hypnotherapist was listed in the Dictionary of Occupational Titles published by the U.S. Department of Labor. There are thousands of trained hypnotists worldwide. Nonetheless, there are organizations actively seeking to limit the free and open practice of hypnosis.

Today, Mesmer's theory of energy being emitted by the healer, which has been long been rejected by modern scientific thought about hypnosis, is resurfacing in the Anewa field of research in subtle energy medicine. Sound, light, magnets, Reiki, Therapeutic Touch, Healing Touch, Reconnection, laying on of the hands, and medical intuition are finding a place in the toolbox of the modern healer. Two centuries after Ben Franklin correctly identified the source of healing as that which comes from the creative imagination, modern psychologists are substantiating the ability of the imagination to prolong life, and enhance the quality of life when dealing with life threatening situations.

Hypnosis is a useful tool for behavior modification, a natural state of relaxation in which optimum learning occurs, and one can perceive the more subtle levels of one's spiritual life. It has been found useful for creative enhancement, weight and pain control, sports improvement, accelerated healing, painless dentistry, natural childbirth, improved study habits and test taking, stress reduction, goal setting and achievement, and overcoming mental or emotional blockages. Olympic and professional athletes routinely use hypnosis to reach more intense, efficient levels of performance. Psychologists, coaches, parents, students, massage therapists, and medical practitioners can benefit from learning to use suggestion more effectively.

You need to understand that hypnosis is a powerful tool for relaxation in a world of increasing speed and complexity.

CHAPTER THREE
UNDERSTANDING HYPNOTHERAPY AND WHAT IT CAN HELP ACHIEVE

Your subconscious mind controls virtually all your thinking. In fact, about 95% of all your thoughts are generated automatically through the unconscious mind. That's exactly the reason for some of our unwanted behaviors. These things have become deeply embedded in our minds as a result of repetition and reinforcements. Many of our fears, anxiety, panic attacks, or vomiting are attributed to this unconscious response. As a therapy, hypnotherapy seeks to reframe and reverse these "habits of thought."

Therefore, hypnotherapy has been shown to be highly effective for a number of unconsciously motivated conditions. Some of the most common include the following:

- **Phobias And Fears**

Hypnosis reframes the fear and untangles the association that keeps that fear in place. Hypnosis can help with fear of flying, driving, heights, the doctor or dentist, insects, intimacy or success.

- **Habits**

Habits are deeply embedded in our thinking due to the repetition and reinforcements. Smokers have numerous triggers such as stress, mealtimes, driving, and boredom, just to name but a few. Hypnosis allows people to examine these unconscious triggers and get rid of them.

Hypnotherapy can help with: smoking, substance abuse, gambling, overeating, and procrastination. Being hypnotized is not dissimilar to being sleepy or in a daydream. Hypnotherapy is simply a method of putting your trance state to work solving your problems. When you're in a hypnotic trance, you are completely aware of the words being spoken to you by the hypnotherapist. And, should a fire alarm go off or any other physically threatening situation arise you will immediately take yourself out of trance to respond.

Hypnosis carries an element of risk as do all therapies and activities. But, as long as your hypnotherapist is properly qualified, and operates within a professional code of conduct and ethics, you needn't worry.

UNDERSTANDING THE DIFFERENCES BETWEEN HYPNOSIS AND HYPNOTHERAPY

It is very important that we know and understand the difference between hypnosis and hypnotherapy. I really need you to understand that there is a big difference between the act of hypnotizing someone (hypnosis) and the amazing changes that can happen with the help of a qualified hypnotherapist (hypnotherapy). I hope that after you read this section you will never confuse a stage hypnotist (the person you see getting laughs on TV) with a hypnotherapist (the person who helps you stop smoking, lose weight, or recover from a life-long phobia).

Hypnosis is a state of mind connected to deep relaxation, narrowed focus, and increased suggestibility. Hypnosis is an intermediate state between sleep and wakefulness.

Hypnosis can be likened to the state you are in when you act intuitively instead of intellectually. During hypnosis, you basically ask your inner drill sergeant to take a break while your clever, artistic self takes the stage. And believe me, everybody has both aspects within them!

Hypnotherapy is hypnosis used for therapeutic purposes. Hypnotherapy applies the technique of hypnosis to encourage your unconscious mind to find solutions to problems.

Hypnosis is a state of consciousness. Hypnotherapy is a therapy. Hypnosis itself is not therapy. The therapy part of a hypnotherapy session occurs after hypnosis has been used to induce your trance. Then the hypnotherapist makes suggestions that help your unconscious mind achieve your goals or remove your problems. Just as there are many avenues to hypnosis, including self-hypnosis and self-induced trances (see the next section), there are many different hypnotherapy techniques and applications.

STAGE HYPNOSIS IS NOT HYPNOTHERAPY

Stage hypnosis is a form of entertainment. It is not a way to receive help for your problems or to achieve your aspirations. I don't recommend that you become personally involved in stage hypnosis as there is no personal care for your individual needs. It's a stage act where the main aim is to get laughs at your expense if you get on stage.

Many people get involved in stage hypnosis with no bad aftereffects. However, some past stage participants have suffered emotional problems afterwards. This is an area of great debate as to whether these people were already predisposed to emotional problems, or if stage hypnosis had a negative influence. You really have to be careful with the type of things you get involved in.

GOING INTO TRANCE

Trance is a state of mind that involves a selective focus of attention. You are in a natural trance state several times each day, usually when you're relaxing.

Examples of times you may slip into a trance include the following:

- Being fully involved in reading a book
- Going window shopping at your favorite stores
- Becoming anxious or fearful about an upcoming event
- Playing with an imaginary friend as a child
- Zoning out while exercising
- Fantasizing about an old love interest

Trance states occur naturally and regularly. Hypnosis utilizes these states to access your unconscious mind in order to help you more easily achieve your goal or solve your problem.

The following are the main trance states, and some of the traits a hypnotized person may experience while in each state, listed from light to deep levels:

Light trance:

Eyes closed, relaxed face muscles, deepened breathing.

Medium trance:

Head and body slump, reduced awareness of surroundings, slower responses, deepening of light trance state.

Deep trance:

Deepening of medium trance state, deeper abdominal breathing.

Somnambulism

A very rare trance state in which a hypnotized person may experience sensations as if awake. Commonly known as sleepwalking, this is a very rare condition. This state is counterproductive in hypnosis because the person is in too deep a state to retain the hypnotherapy suggestions in either their conscious or unconscious memory!

At increasingly deeper levels of trance, you become more open to your unconscious mind and more receptive to hypnotic suggestions from the hypnotherapist.

FINDING HELP WITH HYPNOTHERAPY

Hypnotherapy can help you cope with a wide range of issues, including:

- Increasing your confidence
- Breaking bad habits such as smoking, nail-biting, bed-wetting, and so on
- Removing phobias
- overcome impotence
- increasing sexual libido
- constant feeling of sadness
- public speaking confidence
- Managing or getting rid of pain
- Enhancing performance in artistic, academic, and athletic fields
- Controlling weight and improving eating habits
- Anger Management
- Addictive consumption (e.g. Alcohol, cocaine, gambling)

This is just a brief overview of some of the most common hypnotherapy treatment areas that you can benefit immensely from. If you're curious about a problem not listed here, speaking to a hypnotherapist can certainly clarify whether the issue you're concerned about is one that hypnotherapy can address or not.

UNDERSTANDING THE THERAPEUTIC PART OF HYPNOTHERAPY

I write enthusiastically about the potentials for change that hypnotherapy can provide for you. If you have never experienced hypnotherapy, it's probably a bit difficult to understand how these changes happen when you're in trance, with your eyes closed and in a daydream-like state. Well, that is fair enough.

In order to explain how therapy occurs while you're in trance, remember this: during hypnosis your body is relaxed, but your thoughts become very attentive. You are able to focus at an enhanced level when you are in a hypnotherapy session. And what you are focusing on is the therapist's suggestions. This is where the therapy part begins. If your issue is to avoid sweet, fattening foods, the therapist gives your unconscious mind specific suggestions on how to do this very easily. If you are coming to hypnosis to stop smoking, the hypnotherapist gives you suggestions to remove your associations with smoking, so that you no longer have any desire to smoke and no longer consider yourself to be a smoker.

GOING TO YOUR FIRST HYPNOTHERAPY SESSION

Your very first hypnotherapy session can be an exciting or an intimidating experience, depending on the way and manner that you approach it. It will be exciting if you're prepared and know what to expect. Intimidating if you have fears about hypnosis and are worried about how the session will go.

So what should you expect when you arrive? While specific techniques differ from therapist to therapist, most sessions follow the same general course. In this chapter, we take you through all of the stages of a typical hypnotherapy session, from the first getting-to-know-you questions to the follow-up activities.

A hypnotherapy session really is one of the few things in life that's truly about you. And other than a few common sense items, you don't have to do a great deal of preparation. So relax. Armed with the knowledge in this chapter, you can achieve the best possible results from your hypnosis sessions. Before going for your first hypnotherapy session, there are certain things you must put into consideration so that you will have a great time. Such things include:

- Entering the office

One of the most empowering things to do when you go to your

hypnotherapy session, is to arrive just a bit early. The reason for this is simple: You have a fixed amount of appointment time. Arriving early ensures that you don't waste your money by being late. Besides, being early allows you to relax, compose yourself, and focus on your goals for the session.

Hypnosis is most effective on patients who are able to relax. So find your inner calm and be prepared to see what a difference hypnotherapy can make in your life.

- **Be the one to pay for the services**

Money and session payment are two very interesting subjects for us hypnotherapists. Not only because we pay our mortgage and grocery bills through the fees we collect, but from a motivation perspective. Consider two hypothetical clients:

Joan saved her money for a quit smoking session.

Musa was given the money by his father for a quit smoking session.

Who do you think has the greater chance of success?

It may be unscientific, but it's safe to say that Joan probably has the better shot at quitting smoking than Musa does. In general, self-paying clients tend to be more motivated. This may simply be due to the fact that when you use your own money, you're more highly motivated to get value for it.

When I meet a patient who is not paying for their own therapy, I ask additional questions to determine whether they're motivated. We want to ensure that they aren't being sent to therapy against their own wishes. Because, if that is the case, hypnotherapy is much less likely to be effective for such.

The cost of hypnotherapy varies so much that even stating a ballpark figure would lead to misrepresentation, confusion, and inaccuracy. Hypnotherapists with expensive premises in city centres will charge more than suburban or rural-based therapists. Hypnotherapists who are medically qualified charge differently. There are many possible permutations on fees.

Your hypnotherapist will be happy to tell you his fees, whether you're having a one-off session of a couple of hours, or several sessions over a number of weeks.

- **You Need To Know How Many Sessions It Will Take**

Every hypnotherapist is different, but hypnotherapy is very solution focused. It generally achieves results rapidly compared to most talking therapies. One reason may be that counseling and psychotherapy are concerned with gaining insight, and understanding why you have a problem and what its origins are. Hypnotherapy, on the other hand, is more concerned with obtaining rapid and lasting change than in finding a cause. Gaining insight is a bonus in hypnotherapy, not the goal. Rapid change is the goal, and in my experience, it is exactly what most clients want.

You may wonder how rapid this rapid change is. Well, for example, many hypnotherapists conduct a stop-smoking treatment in a single session. Granted, the session may involve an extended, slightly longer period of 90 minutes being common time duration for a stop-smoking session, as opposed to the normal 50 minutes for all other treatments. The reason for a single stop-smoking session is to give the message that once you're hypnotized to be a non-smoker, subsequent sessions are redundant and actually undermine that message.

However, if you're coming to hypnotherapy with a fairly serious problem; something like an eating disorder, or a problem that is profoundly affecting your quality of life expected anywhere from two to half a dozen sessions and possibly more, depending on the seriousness of the problem.

- **A Good Way To Start Your Hypnotherapy Session**

So are you ready? You booked your first session. What's next?

A hypnotherapy session, rather like most stage presentations, follows a familiar sequence of events with a beginning, middle, and an end. To be sure, some stage presentations mix the sequence up a bit, like Phantom of the Opera, where the curtain rises on a scene years after the masked man finished playing the organ. Of course, if the phantom had undergone hypnotherapy, maybe he wouldn't have had quite so many personal issues . . .

A hypnotherapy session begins, well, at the beginning, probably with introductions and a little small talk to put you at ease. This gentle start not only helps the hypnotherapist establish a good rapport with you, it helps you relax and relaxation is the key to allowing hypnosis to happen.

After the small talk, the hypnotherapist asks you on what issue you want to work. Tell him. Don't be surprised if he tells you that it's an issue he has worked on successfully with other patients. In our experience, most patients do a bit of homework and are familiar with some of the basic areas that hypnotists can work with. After reading this book, you will also be familiar with lesser-known issues hypnosis is effective with.

After that, although therapists may differ slightly in their approach, a single hypnotherapy session typically has specific stages. The rest of this chapter goes into each in detail. No mask or organ music required.

Many hypnotherapists avoid doing any hypnosis during the first session. They may prefer to take a detailed personal history during the initial session. Then again, other hypnotherapists may treat you during your initial session. There really aren't any clear-cut rules about this.

- **How To Get Acquainted With Your Hypnotherapist**

Hypnotherapists are skilled at helping people to relax, so feel free to have a chat with yours. He no doubt already realizes that you may be a bit nervous, or even skeptical of hypnosis. Feel free to tell him exactly how you're feeling and what concerns you have, even if it's that you see hypnotists as strange beings – a cross between a mystic with mind-reading powers and a stage performer. Your honesty helps to get the session underway and helps the hypnotherapist to learn a bit about you and what helps you. The aim is to ensure that you feel comfortable about working with this person. This whole getting acquainted stage should only take a few minutes. In other words, 4 to 5 minutes out of your (most likely) 50-minute session.

- **Creating A Good Working Relationship With Your Hypnotherapist**

Relationships are a big deal to hypnotherapists. Remember that your hypnotherapist is like other helping professionals in that he's genuinely interested in working with you to help you to achieve your goals. The basis for any effective therapeutic relationship is trust. It is important to feel that you can trust your hypnotherapist – always trust your instincts.

By establishing trust, you build rapport with your hypnotherapist. Rapport is a mutual trust and confidence between two people. Yes, rapport is a two-way street – not only do you need to have trust and confidence in your hypnotherapist, but your hypnotherapist needs to feel the same way. The hypnotherapist must feel confident that you're there for the right reasons, that you really want to achieve your goals, and that you can be honest in discussions about your problem. And that you won't do a runner and leave him with an unpaid fee!

Think of rapport as an emotional bridge between you and your hypnotherapist. Effective hypnotherapy begins with building a rapport and making the patient feel respected, welcomed, and reassured that their therapy will be effective. When you have rapport, you have empathy and understanding of how someone's problem may affect their life. This is as important for the hypnotherapist as for the client.

Establishing rapport in any type of personal development work is a crucial part of the therapy. Ample research evidence explains that establishing positive rapport enhances treatment efficacy.

- **Become A Team With Your Hypnotherapist**

If you can approach the work that you are about to do as a joint effort with your hypnotherapist, you have a greater chance of achieving your goals.

Some patients expect the hypnotherapist to do all the work without putting in any effort themselves. It just doesn't work like that folks!

In fact, you can liken you and your therapist to a sports team. You are the excited player, eager to win the game, which may mean overcoming a phobia, or being able to stop smoking. Your hypnotherapist is like a powerful coach, enabling you to unleash inner resources you may have been unaware you possessed. Together, you combine into a powerful unit, ready and able to tackle the toughest opponent.

All hypnosis is a joint effort. This is why we emphasize the need to consider you and your hypnotherapist as a team.

- **Tell Your Hypnotherapist All He Needs To Know**

Your hypnotherapist wants to know how best to help you, so logically he needs to know a little about you before he begins. During your initial session he'll probably ask you a few questions in order to obtain information relevant to your stated problem or goal. This helps him to formulate a treatment plan to determine how best to use hypnosis for you. Some of the questions you're asked are similar to those that other professionals ask at a first meeting. They include:

- Your full name
- Your contact details
- Your date of birth, medical history
- How long you've had the problem
- In what ways you've tried to solve the problem, and the results of these attempts

Taking a case history involves asking about the whole of your life. This may include asking who the members of your immediate family are, getting an overview of your medical history, relationship patterns, your current relationship situation, and discovering whether you have children. Your hypnotherapist may also be interested in any other therapies you've engaged in – counseling, psychotherapy, alternative or complementary treatments, and earlier attempts at hypnotherapy.

Your hypnotherapist may not ask about all of these, but he will try to touch on anything he deems relevant to your current problem.

During the course of this portion, the therapist may ask permission to take notes. First check that his notes remain confidential, and then give him that permission. Notes help the therapist recall important information that enables him to make your sessions more productive. You can assume that information you give is treated as confidential and not shared with any other parties. The only exception is if any incidents of violence towards children arise. In most cases, a confession of violence towards children has to be reported to social services or the police, by law.

CHAPTER FOUR

CONSCIOUS, SUBCONSCIOUS AND SUPERCONSCIOUS

You have five senses through which you perceive and explore the physical world; sight, sound, touch (these are the primary conscious senses), smell and taste (these are the less consciously used senses). Your mind works as a filter. There is so much going on around you that you only consciously pay attention to the parts you are required to or desire to. There is so much information held in your memory banks that you would go crazy if you had to think about all of it. Therefore, your mind distills the incoming information, clumps information, compares it to what is known, and assigns its relevance and storage need based on what you have decided, or been trained, is important. As children, we hear that we use 1/10th of the brain capacity. (What is 100%?) The brain is not the mind. The brain can be sliced and put beneath a microscope. The mind is amorphous. It may be that we are only using 1/10 of 1% of our mind capacity. Ask yourself, what would happen if we used 100%?

When working in hypnosis, we define three states of mind to work with. The conscious mind, the subconscious mind, and the superconscious mind. The conscious state correlates with Sigmund Freud's conscious state. It is the portion of the island image that is visible above the water. The subconscious state correlates with Freud's unconscious state. Hypnosis differs from the Freudian approach with the integration of the superconscious, which can be viewed as the underlying ocean floor, out of which the island rises to peak above the waves. The superconscious is a spiritual aspect of hypnosis has been deliberately omitted from the medical descriptions of what is and is not hypnosis.

Hypnosis is an easy and effective way to change the subconscious mind, bring clarity to the conscious mind, and enhance communication with the superconscious mind. Anything which promotes or facilitates communication with the subconscious, unconscious or superconscious is a form of hypnosis.

THE CONSCIOUS MIND

The conscious mind involves will power and reasoning. It rationalizes data. It is critical and analytical. It has no capacity for emotions. It judges and compares, using polarized thoughts for measurement (hot/cold, wet/dry, light/dark, big/little etc.). This is the critical faculty of the mind. The conscious mind is filled with will power, logic, and reasoning.

THE SUBCONSCIOUS MIND

Broadly speaking, the subconscious mind is powerhouse that has two distinct and unique purposes. They are:

- A will to live which supervises the automatic functions of the body. Through this automatic supervisory capacity, you digest food and eliminate waste products automatically, hair and nails grow automatically, your heart beats, and you breathe even while sleeping. This could be referred to as the engineering department of the mind.

- A vast storehouse which serves as a file system filled with everything you have ever experienced or perceived, including emotions, imagination, decisions, habits and drive. This could be referred to as the secretarial division of the mind.

Using the high speed data bank within, you automatically review what has worked or failed to work in the past, the decisions you made, and the desired outcome you have had. All these happen automatically and so fast that the conscious mind rarely observes the process. The subconscious is the seat of your imagination. Instead of rationalizing in a linear manner, it is emotional, holographical, uncritical, and faithfully records your perceptions and misperceptions. This is the creative engineering department, the imagination, the studio, the lab, the drive, and the habits. It works automatically and impersonally to achieve or impede goals of success and happiness or unhappiness and failure, depending upon the programming you feed into it. That which you are dwelling upon, both positive and negative, are what you are informing your creative self is important and must be tended to. You are pre-conditioned by your environment, past experiences, perceptions, and decisions. Every experience, perception, decision, action and idea is stored in the memory banks of the subconscious. In order to change or modify behavior, the subconscious must be presented with ideas and suggestions, alternatives and perspectives that are reasonable, acceptable and in its best interests.

THE SUPERCONSCIOUS MIND

The superconscious mind involves processes of interconnectedness including species memory, instinct, and genetic code. This amorphous aspect of being contains what Jung called the collective unconscious, archetypes or the collective awareness of a species.

THE AGE LONG BATTLE BETWEEN WILLPOWER AND IMAGINATION

The Battle Between Will Power and Imagination when the subconscious (creativity and imagination) and conscious (logic and willpower) clash, the subconscious mind often always wins. If you decide to consciously hold your breath until you die, you might succeed long enough to pass out, at which time you would automatically start breathing. Getting the subconscious mind working for you instead of against you is a head start on success that you need to note.

WHEN WILL POWER AND IMAGINATION CLASH, THE IMAGINATION OFTEN ALWAYS WINS

Let us consider this example below:

Imagine a plank six inches wide and 20 feet long, laying on the ground. You can walk the length of that board easily. Now imagine placing that same plank 40 feet up in the air. Imagine walking across it now. You may find that you are hesitant to cross the board at that height because an element of uncertainty has entered the situation. Your imagination has recognized the idea, "I might fall." Your will power might force you to walk across, but the imagination is pushing you not to. If there were additional incentives for you to move across such a long, narrow passage, you might find your imagination fully engaged. If you were in a burning building 40 feet up and a plank were extended to you, you would have greater desire to cross the plank because the imagination of burning without trying to save yourself would propel you safely across that plank. When you relearn effective access methods for the imagination, you gain greater awareness and control over the inner workings of your mind.

THE POWER OF THOUGHT

The primary job of your mind is protecting you. Your mind will only allow you to do or perceive what it thinks you are strong enough and ready enough to know or do.

THE UNIVERSE IS MADE OF THOUGHT

There is a thinking stuff from which the universe is made. Your thoughts create movement and form in this thinking stuff, bringing into reality those things you dwell upon within your mind. Your thoughts are energy. You produce energy at 100% output, 100% of the time. You choose how to direct that flow of energy with the way you think. Through hypnosis, you gain greater awareness of your intent, and greater capacity for choosing the direction and force of your applied energy. Hypnosis occurs when the conscious mind is relaxed enough to allow the flow of energy between the superconscious, the subconscious, and the conscious to be clear. The communication of an acceptable idea, its unconscious acceptance, and the subsequent automatic responses and actions are various phases of hypnotic phenomena.

Matter and Energy

There was a time when science broke the known universe into two elements: matter and energy. Then Einstein came along and said there was no such thing as matter, there was only energy vibrating at different frequencies. Bell's Theorem Today, physicists claim that 99% of the universe is invisible to our perceptions. I really don't know how they manage to come to all these conclusions in the first place.

Memory

Your memory is a registration of ideas. For everything you do there is a reason and that reason is created when any two or more ideas are associated. Everything you have learned is stored in your subconscious.

Your driving skill involves memories of getting into your car, maneuvering out onto the freeway, moving into a continuous flow of traffic, and reaching a consistent speed. Often the body has a memory of what needs to be done, and now the conscious mind is free. Because the knowledge required for driving exists in your subconscious, your conscious mind drifts off, allowing your subconscious to become more active. You may become so engrossed in your thoughts that you automatically drive in the direction of your office when your actual destination is somewhere else. You may arrive at your destination and wonder how you got there so quickly. When your attention is needed to change lanes, avoid something in the road, stop at a toll gate, or slow for an off ramp, your conscious mind comes into play, again.

A hypnotist cannot create a picture in the mind of a subject who has never conceived of that particular picture, word, idea or suggestion. By suggestion, the hypnotist illuminates different "frames" in the subject's memory banks. When I say, "Look at this thingamabob," you would not know what it was until I gave more description. "When you put it on a flat surface and spin it, it goes round and round, just like a top." Now you have more information. "It is a flat piece of metal with a little indentation and a reflective surface and it spins for a long time." Now you have a more complete picture. Once I show you this thingamabob, you will understand it even more. When you hold it, spin it and play with it yourself, you have greater comprehension of the limits and capacities of the thingamabob. The next time I mention that flat, spinning thingamabob, you have a set of ideas which correspond to my thingamabob. Be sure you practice the exercises in this program, so that you gain experiential awareness of these processes, thereby engaging your own mind in the process of life affirming growth.

CHAPTER FIVE

THE POWER OF SUGGESTION

It is your natural ability to respond to suggestion that enables you to harness the full power of the mind. Every person has an ability to respond to suggestion; some are more suggestible than others.

Want it to Happen (Desire / Intent)

Watch it Happen (Creative Visualization / Dream Induction)

Allow it to Happen (Do the best you can each and every day with what you have at hand.)

Ideas

An idea is something that stimulates or suggests something to one sense. Thoughts are combinations of ideas. Comprehension generally occurs once an idea stimulates three senses.

A THREE STEP LEARNING PATTERN

It takes the average adult at least three experiences for learning:

- The first time an idea is presented, the average individual discards the idea as foreign.
- The second time an idea is presented; the individual discovers a vague familiarity either before or after discarding the idea.
- The third time an idea is presented, the individual recognizes the idea as familiar, and may retrieve the previous two memories to compare.

SUGGESTIBILITY VS GULLIBILITY

You should know that suggestible is different from gullible in so many ways as I will explain further. Suggestible individuals are open to suggestions, while keeping in mind their own objectives. Suggestibility can be equally powerful for growth and destruction. The individual who utilizes ongoing positive, powerful, empowering verbal and nonverbal suggestions incorporates them into peak positive performance. An underachiever utilizes ongoing negative verbal and nonverbal suggestions, incorporating them into life denying experiences of peak underachievement. Both the over and the underachiever are hypnotizing themselves into their state of being outside of the norm for a male or female of that age and culture.

A gullible person tends to have poor judgment, poorly developed critical faculty, and allows him or herself to be sucked into something he or she doesn't really want. A suggestible person has excellent judgment and an ability to suspend the functioning of the critical faculty when desired. A common myth about hypnosis is that only the weak willed or weak minded can be hypnotized. It is more common to find that the more intelligent the subject, the better the response to suggestions perceived to be beneficial, fun, helpful, and addressing the subject's innermost longings. The more aware the subject is, the better the response. Some think that the stronger the will, the greater the concentration, the better the long term results. This program of self regulation is intended to bring congruent alignment between the inner emotional power, and the outer will and awareness. When there is congruence between the inner and outer capacities of a human, it is easier to achieve objectives given a supportive environment with a goodness of fit.

HOW PEOPLE RESPOND TO SUGGESTIONS

You determine the level of your response to suggestion at any given time. People respond to suggestion differently and some people are more responsive than others. You are always aware at some level and have the power to accept or reject any suggestion. The ability to respond changes from moment to moment depending on your state of being and the environment. Once a suggestion is accepted, it can take hold two ways; instantly or gradually. A suggestion can also be rejected if the critical faculty intervenes in comparative analysis, or to reject an idea as irrelevant or detrimental to the well being of the individual.

- **Instantly Accepting Suggestions**

You may notice immediate response to the suggestion. Some people have such a strong desire for response that they steam roll right over the slow hypnotist. Some subjects are in trance as soon as they enter the office. This is particularly true when the subject is entering a hospital or medical clinic. Environment and emotional states can induce trance, so each of us experiences different degrees of suggestibility at different times. People don't require formal trance induction to experience hypnosis or respond to suggestions. Depth is not required for a suggestion to be effective.

- **Gradually Accepting Suggestions**

You may notice response after time or after repeated stimulation, this is known as compounding or stacking suggestions.

Each suggestion accepted creates a foundation for the acceptance of the next suggestion. Start with the small suggestions, those easy to achieve, and build upon them, one simple statement on top of another. Another method for gradual change and response to suggestion is to deliver open ended suggestions, such as those made popular by Emile Couie, "Every day in every way, I am getting better and better and better."

TAKING RESPONSIBILITY

You, the subject, are responsible for the way you think and respond to suggestion. You chose to utilize or reject each suggestion. You cannot be made to do anything that is against your personal, moral or religious beliefs, solely by the power of suggestion. You have to be willing, wanting, and strongly desirous. The level of desire is generally in direct proportion to the level of response. Taking responsibility means paying attention to your senses and your ability to respond.

YOUR INNER LIE DETECTOR

This exercise is designed to bring awareness of your feelings, a kinesthetic awareness of your bodily response to a particular stimulation, or suggestion, to your conscious mind. When your body is agreeing with something, it usually has a positive physical or kinesthetic response. When your body is disagreeing with a particular stimulation, or suggestion, it usually has a negative physical or kinesthetic response.

You should always pay attention to the feelings in the middle of the body, particularly from the sternum to about two inches below the belly button. You may want to place a hand on the diaphragm or belly to draw your attention there. Breathe deeply. There is a part deep in the middle of your body that knows truth and false. It is a feeling self that you have experienced many times. Let's call it the abdominal brain. You know what is true and false in your head, you've consciously trained that part. The abdominal area digests everything, not just physical food, it also digests mental, emotional and spiritual food. Some things are not food, are not digestible and recognized by the gut feelings as false, poison or distasteful. When attended to, this gut instinct can help reject negative experiences or options. During the next exercise, pay close attention to what you perceive occurring in the middle of your body, or any other body changes that are your personal body awareness of truth and false. Now say to yourself:

"I am a woman." (And notice how you feel in your body.)

"I am a man." (And notice how you feel in your body.)

Notice the difference between your body feeling of truth and false. If you have no sensation of difference, it may indicate that you are balanced in your male and female aspects. Perhaps you are numb or detached. Go on to the next two statements:

"I am breathing in air." (Notice how you feel in the body.)

"I am breathing in charcoal dust." (Notice how you feel in the body.)

The previous exercise can be done anywhere, anytime, to help you reconnect with your inner knowing, by deliberately lying to yourself about something and noticing how you feel about it, and then correcting yourself with your perception of truth and, again, noticing how you feel about it.

BELIEFS

Humans tend to believe certain things about themselves. Things are suggested by parents, peers, educators, authorities, spouses, environment, etc. Individuals then choose to use or discard the incoming suggestions, based on what is believed about self, relationships, and the surrounding world. This reality is reflected in verbal and non-verbal communication. The beliefs set the pattern for what is thought and done, effectively screening out information that doesn't fit the existing beliefs. The underlying assumptions of beliefs are the values enculturated by the individual's family, cultural, temporal, and geographic systems.

SELECTIVE THINKING

The individual seeking hypnosis is in need. Often the first need is relaxation. This makes the hypnotist's job easy, as the one thing all people have in common when practicing the hypnosis of this course is relaxation. The body generally responds quickly to suggestions of well being. As soon as the subject's attention is redirected with simple suggestions of relaxation, the subject's critical faculty has been bypassed and selective thinking (relaxation) is established. Suggestions built upon previously accepted suggestions create greater response to the earlier suggestions, a compounding effect that can be further augmented with truisms about reality. Layering and compounding suggestions for well being establish a selective thinking of good rapport and acceptance of suggestions, compounded by every suggestion accepted. As positive ideas are layered into your awareness, there is often a corresponding positive shift that occurs in your overall well being. Becoming relaxed, becoming aware, an expanded awareness of open heart and relaxed mind can be a pleasant unfolding of self.

THE BEST WAY TO DELIVER SUGGESTIONS

A suggestion must be given with complete confidence and assurance. Lock your mind around the idea of your suggestions being accepted and acted upon by the subject receiving the suggestions. If room for doubt creeps in, that message of uncertainty will be delivered to the subject, and may render any affiliated suggestion ineffective as the subject reestablishes critical thinking. Suggestion must be delivered with the same assurance as if it has happened, is happening or is, without a doubt, going to happen, just as surely as the sun rises and sets. Speak confidently and create a picture in your own mind of what it is that you desire actually occurring before and during giving suggestion. In this way, you speak with the confidence of a person who perceives clearly and trusts his or her natural inner vision, hears the inner voice and speaks clearly using the inner voice, sees clearly with the inner vision. Deliver your suggestions in a natural manner, just as you would naturally speak about observing the moon rise or the sun set.

Many people have hypnotic voices. It comes from speaking confidently, with a voice supported with breathing from the diaphragm. Breathing exercises such as the pranayama of yoga and singing lessons are helpful. Pace the words you start with using a rhythmic pattern that is comfortable to you. Perhaps pace the words with the breathing of the subject. Match and mirror the vocal patterns of the subject. Some hypnotists elect to use monotony to bore the conscious mind and drive its attention elsewhere. As soon as the subject=s conscious mind loses interest in paying attention to you and your predictable, boring suggestions of relaxation, it wanders away to more interesting ideas. At this point, the subject may notice a duality of the inner voice, as if they are hearing more than one idea at a time. It may become an experience of noticing layers upon layers upon layers of ideas. This is excellent response. Some people describe the experience of the mind wandering away from the words of the hypnotist as being similar to the fading in and out of a radio with sporadic reception.

As you present your suggestions of relaxation, watch for the signs of hypnosis. When you notice the signs, begin to deliver the suggestions for the relief requested by the subject with present tense, ongoing present to future tense, personal empowerment, and focused on positive outcomes toward which one is moving. Encourage the subject with suggestions:

"That's it. Stay with that feeling of relaxation. Trust yourself. You can you know. Breathe deep and easy. Breathe only as much as you need to sustain your body perfectly. You know more about you than anyone else ever will. You know what you need to FEEL BETTER, trust yourself. Relax deep and easy. You know you can TRUST YOURSELF TO RELAX COMPLETELY."

PRE-HYPNOTIC SUGGESTION (THE PRETALK)

Pretalk is like getting an instruction manual and reading it before using something. The pretalk is crucial for you. Here is where you dislodge any previously incorrect ideas about hypnosis and educate the subject to correctly recognize this natural phenomenon called hypnosis. Educating the subject is important for good hypnosis experiences. Tell the subject, in advance, what they can expect to experience. This is a building of expectancy, on top of the expectancy of a person who has specifically come seeking hypnosis for general curiosity or specific objectives. Within any group, large or small, there will be variation in response. There will always be those who refuse to respond at this moment. That doesn't mean they can't be hypnotized, it simply means that they do not wish to experience that particular aspect of self regulation at this time. That's fine. Once they know what to look for, they may find it easier to respond when they are ready to explore it outside of its natural role in going to sleep and waking up from sleep. The purpose of the pretalk is to create a language structure to describe a natural phenomenon which has been used by that human for years, often without an ability to articulate exactly what is being experienced or done.

BEING IN THE MOMENT

You can deepen the rapport you have with your subject, along with the subject's state of being, by commenting on what is occurring. Speaking truisms helps deepen trust. Tell the subject what is happening as it is happening, encourage them to continue doing what they are already doing, and add affirmations of well being to boost the feelings of well being.

"That's right . . . and good . . . relaxing more with every breath . . . noticing how good it feels to relax . . . letting everything go . . . like a puffy cloud floating away on a clear blue sky . . . being full present with each breath, and how good it all feels to be fully connected, in the skin, relaxed and aware."

POST-HYPNOTIC ANALYSIS

Once the experience is complete, discuss what happened.

"Now tell me about that."

"Kind of surprised yourself? Tell me about that."

"Is there anything that sticks out from your experience that you would like to share with me?"

"Is there anything you found particularly interesting?"

"Is there anything you observed or experienced that sticks out for you?"

This allows the subject to comment on anything he or she found particularly interesting or disturbing, and allows him or her to develop more familiarity with his or her ability to respond to suggestion. Often, the longer you wait between experiencing hypnosis and discussing what happened, the more common it is for the subject to have less and less recall of the experience.

COMPOUNDING SUGGESTIONS

Once selective thinking is established, the effects of suggestions begin to compound. Every suggestion that is accepted causes every subsequent suggestion to find easier acceptance. For each additional suggestion that is accepted, the effects of the previous suggestions become more pronounced. The suggestion being delivered can be the same suggestion over and over. Repetition drums things into your head. Through this repetition, advertising finds its greatest success. Every time you hear something it becomes more familiar. One way politicians get their incumbent steam is through name familiarity. Even if a name is familiar because of bad press, people tend to go for the familiar.

Another way suggestion is compounded is by layering suggestion on top of suggestion.

"Go deeper into droopy, drowsy slumber as your eyelids get heavy and close and you go deeper into the knowing."

These are three distinct ideas being delivered at the same time. The first is droopy, drowsy slumber. The second is the eyelids get heavy and close. The third is you go deeper into the knowing.

The use of and, as, and but correlates the ideas into one thought.

The eyes generally blink with each new thought.

Implied messages are wonderful tools for compounding the effects of suggestion.

This suggestion could also be phrased, "Breathe deep and easy." As a hypnotist, taking the simple ideas, and layering them upon each other creates a complexity that overloads the conscious mind and delivers messages directly to the emotional, unconscious or subconscious aspects of mind. Every suggestion that is accepted by the mind lays a foundation for acceptance of subsequent suggestions. With each subsequent suggestion that is delivered, the previous suggestions gain strength. Stretching out the concepts, fleshing them in imaginatively, allows the voice and words to begin steering the mind to the subjective world of natural or organic response, a world slower than the pace set by modern technology, mass media and entertainment.

Anything I do will increase your (relaxation, numbness, forgetfulness, studying, test taking, awareness, sporting performance, anesthesia . . . etc.). Anything can be used to compound a suggestion. A body movement, word, situation, just about anything at all. The desire for relaxation and the welcome suggestions of well being stimulate the mind to create rapid results, recreating balance, ease, calm and well being. The first suggestion may be weak, but when it is compounded with another suggestion, even a totally different suggestion, the first one becomes stronger. When another suggestion is added, the first two suggestions get stronger and so on.

POST HYPNOTIC SUGGESTION

A post hypnotic suggestion is any suggestion delivered in trance and carried out after trance has been formally ended. A post hypnotic suggestion may have immediate response, or a delayed response, or no response. It is up to the innermost desires of the individual receiving the suggestion to act upon, or discard, the incoming stimulation.

WAKING SUGGESTION

Waking suggestions are suggestions given during normal waking consciousness. When formal induction is not used prior to delivering suggestion, you are dealing with waking suggestion. Response to suggestion is not limited to a hypnotic or trance state, depth is not required for excellent or even minor responses to suggestion. The bridge between the inner world and the outer world occurs many times daily. As soon as the critical and analytical factors are bypassed, the mind is refocused and the flow of life energy (emotion and thought) is redirected.

A child with a cut knee runs to mom or dad who kisses it to make it better. Within minutes, the child is running about playing with friends, again. The child did not analyze and question the suggestion and subsequent act, the selective thinking was established that as soon as mom or dad kissed the knee, it would feel better, and so it felt better.

Waking hypnosis is achieved when:

- The mind has locked itself around a given idea.
- The suggestion is acceptable to the subject.

Waking suggestion can be observed in advertising, politics, parenting, education, business and any other endeavor in which humans interact with the environment, others and self. Today, as you are reading these words, you are redirecting your attention and enriching your understanding of self.

Someone yawning in a room gives the other occupants of the room the unspoken suggestion of yawning and increasing the oxygen in the body. The urge to YAWN is a simple suggestion and your response to the suggestion indicates your level of suggestibility (ability to respond to suggestion) AT THIS MOMENT. The suggestion to yawn is a visual waking suggestion. If you have experienced an urge to yawn in response to reading about yawning, or hearing the word yawn, or hearing the sound of a yawn, you may have experienced either a memory of seeing someone else yawn or a memory of yourself yawning, or both. The memory of seeing someone yawn is a positive visual hallucination. The memory of yawning is a positive kinesthetic hallucination. If you experienced either of these memories, or just responded with an automatic yawn or big sigh, you are highly suggestible to waking suggestions. You may need to learn to pay close attention to what kind of suggestions you let in through advertising, television, and written material.

WAKING TRANCE

Many people, as they enter a hospital, enter trance. They are getting ready for the ideas of an expert to instruct them. Thus when a doctor gives a placebo, he or she is using waking suggestion, compounded by the waking trance of the patient.

On a hot day, if someone casually states how hot it is, you might, shortly thereafter, notice how hot it is.

Perhaps someone comments on how wonderful you look, and you may find you respond by perking up and feeling a bit sparklier.

All of the above scenarios are examples of waking trance, in which you have received and responded to a waking suggestion. These suggestions alone do not precipitate a waking state of hypnosis. You first have to accept the suggestion. This can occur two ways:

- By agreeing and letting the idea in,
- By failing to disagree.

REJECTING SUGGESTIONS

Inside each person is a knowing. It knows everything about that person and it knows that it knows. The subject will reject any suggestion that is detrimental to him or her or that goes against strongly held personal, moral or religious beliefs. It is the hypnotist's job to help the subject reestablish a sense of self trust. The subject knows what he or she needs. Awareness of the inner knowing realigns the subject's experiences with their own sense of centeredness and balance. The subject will selectively choose which suggestions to use. All this comes from trusting one's senses and perceptions. When an idea is rejected, one of several things occurs. The subject may:

- Ignore the suggestion and move on to the next idea, suggestion or behavior,
- shut down on any further suggestion,
- Implant their own suggestion in the gap left by the rejected suggestion, or
- Hear the suggestion the way they wanted to hear it.

When providing subjects with audio tapes of their sessions, they will often say that each they hear it, they something entirely different.

GREAT WAYS TO PROGRAM OR REPROGRAM YOUR SUBCONSCIOUS

- **Repetition**

Given sufficient time, repetition is an excellent tool for learning. The amount of time or repetition varies from person to person. This is easily observed through the practice used to created good musicians, athletes, typists, mathematicians, and any other skill which improves with practice, and repetition.

- **Identification**

We long to find others like ourselves. We emulate people we admire in order to become more like them. Our peers pressure us to conform. We link ourselves ethnically. Advertisers appeal to our desire to be sexier, healthier, wealthier, smarter and more attractive by implying that their product with bring us the desired results, and often use well known people to promote their products.

- **Authority**

Much of what we know is programmed into us as children by our parents, teachers and other authority figures. When we hold someone in high esteem, much of what they say goes directly into the subconscious. The subconscious mind, and most children, don't judge things as right or wrong, good or bad. Information from authority is often incorporated, without question, as reality.

- **Emotions**

When we are emotional, the subconscious mind is wide open for new programming. Pay attention to the impressions you are feeding yourself. It is easier to produce a positive result, from a positive emotion or thought. The only person in charge of your thoughts and emotions is you. There may be certain people or situations that push your buttons, but you can decide to buy into or detach from the emotional load.

CHAPTER SIX

FORMULATING POSITIVE SUGGESTIONS

Your perceptions effect your decisions and actions. Anything that can be perceived creates ideas, suggestions for things you may experience, do, or think. Successful suggestions create perceptual arousal that lead to some form of response. Your thoughts are generally not put into action until at least two senses are stimulated. When a series of perceptions connect to form a thought, the thought can lead to action in which each idea in its proper place is certain to appear and it is beyond the power of the individual to resist it. For example, when you read, "Think of a horse," you may have a variety of perceptual memories that comprise a horse. Its form, smell, and sound may flash so quickly through the inner images that you do not notice them consciously, or you may leisurely savor your perceptual memories and stimulations regarding the word horse. The word "horse" is only a word symbol for your perceptual aware of a horse. Effective suggestion requires that you have some common foundation of semantics, and capacity for rapport so as to formulate effective, productive suggestions.

Once you have clearly defined your goals for the session, the hypnotist helps the you paint a picture on the canvas of his or her mind with the power of suggestion. The words, of them self, may arouse no action. The environment, the tone of voice used, the expression on the speaker's face, and body movements all influence thought. These non-verbal communication skills tend to create easier communication patterns among people of the same culture, and a potential for miscommunication cross culturally, and intergenerationally. The more one senses congruity in words and actions, the greater the ability to trust and rapidly respond to the incoming ideas and suggestions. Saying "yes" while shaking one's head "no" is incongruent.

As you paint a picture in your mind, words and actions, comment on what you perceive with your senses. Natural phenomenon are truisms, common and shared perceptions that can help you establish and maintain rapport. Comment on shared perceptions. Hypnotists make use of truisms to establish and deepen rapport between them and their clients. Hypnotists help the individual learn to trust his or her perceptions, identifying and understanding subtle behavioral and cognitive patterns.

While giving suggestions, I give the subject complete focus of my attention as best you can. The focus of attention creates a powerful rapport. This focus is more commonly found in moments of intense emotion. Few people willingly devote such focused attention to another person, other than a mother. I will lead you gently through your own response to relaxation, ask questions, solicit feedback and mirror the subject to enhance the subject's experience. Your mind has already been receiving suggestions, followed by suggestions, compounding the effects of all suggestions given. The goal is for you to be so deeply into what they are doing that you rarely notice when your direct command is of, "You will try to . . . (open your eyes/open your hands/bend that arm) . . . and you cannot.

HOW TO DEVELOP EFFECTIVE SUGGESTIONS

The sole purpose of affirmations and suggestions is to help your subconscious conceive of, believe in and achieve your goals. Developing positive suggestions can help motivate and boost your energy and self esteem, with a focus on life affirming thoughts and actions. Negative suggestions are equally powerful in disrupting healthy activities and thoughts within you. As you learn to hypnotize yourself and others, you benefit from learning how to phrase your words with positive affirmations. Positive affirmations are positive statements of beliefs; powerful tools that can help you create success attitudes in your subconscious. Opening to your creative subconscious with positive affirmations helps you learn to harness the enhanced gifts of your creative imagination in ways productive for you.

- **Use Positive Statements**

State what you want, instead of what you don't want. Take a moment to envision your desired outcomes, the solutions, rather than the problem itself.

- **Awareness Is Important**

Whatever you are most aware of is what you attract. When you put mental energy into something, you tend to find it everywhere. Use your affirmations to focus on the result you desire, or the method of attaining the results, rather than the problem. - I am in control of my appetite. (incorrect - this sounds harmless, but it claims an appetite that needs controlling.) + I eat as much as I need to sustain my body perfectly. (correct)

- **Use the Present Tense**

I will diet until I lose weight is incorrect because it gives you the opportunity to do it later and it implies that you are losing something. You may trick yourself into letting yourself lapse today by this wording. I am more and more slender each and every day is the best statement because it makes your conscious mind to know that this suggestion is future based, but present improved. The subconscious can make is comfortable use of open ended life affirming ideas.

- Be Specific and Intentional

Carefully state exactly what you desire, avoiding slang or wording with multiple meanings. I am losing 20 pounds is incorrect because your mind goes nuts when I lose things. You wouldn't to lose weight and find it again. You must shed, reduce, discard, take off, eliminate, get rid of, and throw away. Each and every day, I am closer to my goal of _____ weigh or size.

- Use "I Am"

Identify who is doing what. Be sure to include yourself. The action, behavior, thoughts, feelings, and responsibilities are things for you to do or experience, not something you want someone else to do.

HOW TO EDIT YOUR AFFIRMATIONS

When you have written your affirmations, be sure that you

have been specific and written in the present tense. Once you have corrected any wording errors, enter self hypnosis and relax for several minutes before reviewing you affirmations, again. Discard any affirmations that make you feel uncomfortable. Affirm the method as well as end result. Affirm proper attitudes and your own personal beliefs in the attainment of your goals. You can bypass the logical arguments against your goals by using ideomotor finger response to confirm your choices of affirmations.

A Sample Affirmations for Weight Reduction

I am more relaxed with myself. I am more aware of my feelings. I express myself with the appropriate feelings. I desire to attain and maintain the best weight for my body. I am more and more comfortable with myself and I am worth it. Each and every day, I am more and more aware of my own beauty. Every day in every way I am thinking and acting and moving toward my proper weight, growing more and more comfortable with myself and all my uniqueness. I eat just enough food to sustain my body perfectly. I listen to my body and give it the mental, physical, emotional or spiritual food it desires. I trust myself more each and every day. I am enjoying how my body feels when I exercise, perhaps walking, or swimming, riding a bike or dancing, going to the gym or going about my daily affairs in ways that are healthy and good for my body. As I discover myself becoming more comfortable with a sustainable and enjoyable diet and exercise, every day in every way it is easier to reach and maintain my proper weight. I now enjoy foods that are good for my body. I am more and more satisfied with myself. I eat only what I need to sustain my body perfectly because I am worth it. I am responsible for my thoughts, feelings, words and actions. As my slender image becomes more and more real in my mind, my slender image becomes more and more real in my body. I find myself enjoying the moments of exercise I get throughout the day as I go about my daily affairs, and take breaks for movement and exercise that help me feeling more limber and relaxed in my body. Today I choose to be myself and enjoy myself, more and more relaxed each and every day.

POST HYPNOTIC SUGGESTIONS

There are two types of post hypnotic suggestions and they include the following:

- Response projected or continued into the waking state.
- Response elicited from sudden signal or subconscious message or stimulus.

See an example of a projected post hypnotic suggestion

"That's fine. When you emerge from trance, and return to full waking state, you will remember to forget all about _____."

Another projected example

"That's fine, as I count from five to one, you will return to full waking state feeling better than you felt before, better than you have felt in a long time, remembering to forget those things you don't need to remember."

See an elicitation example:

"That's fine, close your eyes. When I have you open your eyes, any time you see me _____ / hypnotic trigger / you will instantly _____ / post hypnotic suggestion /. You won't remember that I gave you this suggestion but you will react to it. You can forget consciously this whole conversation, but any time I ___ / hypnotic trigger /, you are going to ___/ post hypnotic suggestion /. It will happen instantaneously. You won't remember that I gave this suggestion. Forget the whole conversation, but be guided by it. All right, now open your eyes, please. How do you feel?

CHAPTER SEVEN

THE THINGS THAT INFLUENCE YOUR ABILITY TO RESPOND

Pretalk

It is important to discuss the subject's previous experience(s) with hypnosis. Dispel the myths of hypnosis. The primary interference with a good response to hypnosis is fear and related lack of trust. Generally the fear is nothing more than a fear of the unknown. Sometimes it may be a fear of change. Fears must be identified and released for you to experience to feel the benefits of hypnosis and for good rapport to occur. You need to start with relaxing and trusting yourself.

Use progressive relaxation. If this is unsuccessful, use suggestibility tests to open the door to the subconscious and use whichever test gives the best response as the induction. Every person has a unique quality of response to hypnosis. Some people pick up hypnosis faster than others. Use direct suggestion to offer yourself a choice in how much time you want to invest in learning how to more fully utilize their innate gifts of learning and health.

"Some people get their benefits in one session. Such persons are always ready; they rapidly assimilate the tools offered to their own best advantage and achieve their desired results in one session. Some people require two to six sessions to respond well to hypnosis. These people sometimes encounter minor setbacks, obstacles or blocks to an immediate response, but after a short period of training, they have the hang of relaxation as a self awareness tool, a tool of change. Some people take a long time to achieve their goals, some take just a year while others take longer time. Through patience and persistence, these people, too, achieve their goal(s). Some people are out to prove that no one can make them change. They are absolutely correct. They will prove them self correct every time and it is a waste of time to attempt to convince them until they change their mind. Change can only occur with the subject has decides that change is possible and it is something they strongly desire.

THREE IMPORTANT THINGS NECESSARY FOR HYPNOSIS TO OCCUR

There are many things that can affect a person's ability to respond to suggestion in any given situation. Every Normal person is hypnotizable. When you want to be hypnotized you must do three things. You must do the following:

- Want to be hypnotized;
- Trust the hypnotist (and self);
- Be free from any fears of hypnosis

MENTAL EXPECTANCY

A visual demonstration of the state has tremendous value in assisting others in the exploration of hypnosis. When working with groups, use the most responsive subjects to first demonstrate the exercises you will be using on the other members of the group. This establishes expectancy quickly. Fascination and curiosity are excellent tools to augment the response to suggestion. Respect from and for the operator is imperative. Emotions can enhance or destroy rapport. Distrust and dislike are not favorable. Anger, fear and a desire for revenge can block the ability to respond to suggestion. Sadness can be a door into the subconscious for therapeutic work, but ungrieved sorrow can also be a barrier to success. Joy, happiness, love all enhance the quality of response to suggestion.

AMBIANCE

- **Temperature**

Too much heat or cold is detrimental to good response. Cold breezes or drafts are detrimental. A temperature slightly on the warm side is preferable. Cold hands and skin need to be addressed for most favorable response.

- **Sound**

It is handy to have a quiet soothing environment, but this is not absolutely necessary. Some people report that background sounds are distracting. Others say that they don't even notice the background sounds. Others say they hear the background sounds, but they are unimportant. Some people enjoy background music. Some enjoy sounds of nature. Some prefer quiet. Headphones and a lapel microphone are handy for creating a quiet space.

When working in loud areas, be an opportunist, use the sound disruptions as deepening tools with suggestions like, all background sounds send you deeper, or, Every time you become aware of any background sounds, it assures you all is well in the outside world, and you go deeper.

- **Light**

Quiet or subdued light is good for most subjects. Some subjects prefer a dimmed room, with sunlight or bright artificial light creating a hindrance to full relaxation.

- **Color**

Light blues, purples and soft greens are thought to be spiritual enhancers. Red, orange and yellow are thought to stimulate the animal grounding, the animal knowing. You can use color and light to set the mood of the environment, and to stimulate non-logical therapeutic results.

- **Smell**

Fragrance has a powerful effect. What one person considers strong unpleasant odors, another may find helpful. Strong, sweet or pleasant odors can be helpful in some cases, distracting in others. Incense reminds some people of the occult or drugs and is undesirable to them. For others, incense is religious or inspirational.

- **Physical Comfort**

The body enjoys relaxation. Good physical support for the head, neck and body enhances the relaxation. Loose clothing is good. Have the subject remove or loosen any tight fitting clothing or accessories. Hands and legs need to be comfortable. Working with a subject who is intoxicated, drunk or high, is less desirable as the mind and mood altering substances can create a barrier to good rapport.

CHAPTER EIGHT

UNDERSTAND THAT HYPNOTHERAPY HAS ITS LIMITATIONS

You are considering sorting out a problem by paying a visit to a hypnotherapist. Before you do, I suggest that you mull over a few things about the responsibilities of that hypnotherapist, as well as some of the realities of hypnotherapy itself. After all, you want to go in for therapy with realistic expectations and a clear understanding of what to expect from your therapist and the process itself. The information in this chapter gives you just that.

The truth is that hypnotherapy is not magic and hypnotherapists do not have special powers. You're not going to walk in for a hypnotherapy session and walk out an hour or so later with all your cares and woes miraculously cured, hallelujah!

Many myths surround hypnotherapy and many people walk into a session expecting the impossible. When you go for therapy, enter into it with realistic expectations. That means understanding what can be done and what can't be done. It can be a great help to you in the long run.

Cure is a word often misused by patients and by some hypnotherapists. Cure implies that something is going to go away. Possibly for good and never come back. Oh, how I wish therapy were that simple. Unfortunately, it isn't, and it never will be. No hypnotherapist worth his or her salt will promise a cure to his or her patients because he or she cannot guarantee that the problem you work on will go away. It may; or you may learn to live more comfortably with it; or it may go away and return at a later date; or it may be that nothing changes at all. All these possible outcomes apply to any form of therapy or medical procedure. You may be thinking 'What's the point in going for therapy then, if there's no guarantee of change?' The fact of the matter is that no therapy can guarantee change. However, hypnotherapy does have an excellent track record and the evidence shows it to be very effective at helping people to make positive changes to their lives and to achieve their goals.

Hypnotherapy helps. That means it is an aid to overcoming something, and as such, relies on the effort you are prepared to put into the therapy process. It can't do it all on its own.

YOU MUST LEARN TO ACCEPT THE LIMITATIONS OF HYPNOTHERAPY

When you go for your hypnotherapy session you need to be realistic about what it can achieve. Although hypnotherapy's effects are wide-ranging, like any other therapy approach it does have its limitations. As with anything and everything, many factors determine the outcome of hypnotherapy: Such factors include the following:

YOUR SYMPTOM

Hypnotherapy can help resolve many different symptoms. However, it cannot help with everything. The chapters in Parts 2 and 3 of this book give you a good idea as to the type of symptoms that can and can't benefit from hypnotherapy. For example, cigarette addiction can be treated, whereas the treatment of heroin addiction should be left to the medical profession. If in doubt, ask your therapist if hypnotherapy is right for your symptom.

Your symptom itself often determines the length of time you spend in therapy. Smoking cessation can take as little as one session to complete. However, if you are being treated for something more involved, such as bulimia, you can expect a longer course of treatment because of the deeper issues involved with this condition and its treatment.

YOUR EXPECTATIONS

Are you expecting too much from hypnotherapy? Do you think it is a magical panacea that will get rid of your symptom at the click of a finger?

The 'I want to lose two stone by Friday' mindset is doomed to failure. Your expectations must be realistic from the outset. Hypnotherapy is therapy, not magic! Discuss your expectations with your therapist and be prepared to have the reality of the process pointed out to you.

So what can you realistically expect from hypnotherapy? You can expect to have a very good chance at relieving your symptom. As with any course of treatment, medical or not, you can't have an absolute guarantee that the treatment will work. Why? Because of the factors we discuss here.

You can also expect to put some effort into your therapy process by carrying out homework assignments that continue the therapy process, even when you are not with your therapist. You can also expect that your therapist will put in as much time and effort as is needed to help you overcome your symptom.

YOUR FEARS

Are you at ease with your hypnotherapy session? Do you fear

anything about the process you're going through, such as whether the effects of your therapy will be long-lasting, or just how effective it will be? Perhaps you're worried that you aren't going into trance in the way that you thought you would. Maybe you're concerned that being in trance now will affect you during the meeting you're chairing later in the day.

If these or any other fears spring to mind during your therapy session, discuss them with your therapist before, during – yes, you can talk in trance – or after the trance has concluded, and let her put your mind at ease. Letting such fears fester away without discussing them interferes with your chances of having a good outcome for your therapy.

YOUR RELATIONSHIP WITH THE HYPNOTHERAPIST

Is it a good one? Do you feel comfortable with her? Is your therapist someone you can work with? Like any relationship, the better it is, the smoother things run. If you don't feel comfortable with, or dislike, your therapist for any reason, the all-important trust factor will not be there. If you don't trust your therapist then your mind won't trust the therapy process itself. If this is the case, then politely say 'Thanks, but no thanks' to your therapist, and find another in whose company you do feel comfortable. Remember, the therapy sessions are for you, not your therapist.

What's going on in your life at the moment: Life has its ups and downs and these may help or hinder your therapy. If all is hunky-dory and good things are happening in your life, you tend to feel upbeat, positive, and motivated – you have what's known as a positive mindset. These good feelings affect the way you view the course of your therapy, making you more optimistic, positive, and motivated about the whole process and its outcome. With this positive mindset you could very well find that your unconscious mind is more open to the suggestions your hypnotherapist is giving; speeding up the process of change.

DO NOT GO YET; ONE LAST THING TO DO

If you enjoyed this book or found it useful I'd be very grateful if you'd post a short review on Amazon. Your support really does make a difference and I read all the reviews personally so I can get your feedback and make this book even better.

Thanks again for your support!

ABOUT THE AUTHOR

www.yourfuture.es - www.digitalhumans.es

For round about 14 years I've been professionally active as a **Senior Recruitment / Talent Acquisition Manager** and **Senior Change Manager** with a focus on *Digital Transformation* in the areas of **HR and Recruitment**.

I'm used to quickly and precisely adjusting to people and to attentively listen to them. As an expert in the field of Digital Transformation, I am aware of the unbelievable speed of market demands towards people.

Over the past five years I have increasingly experienced the struggle of many companies for the best of employees in order to remain competitive in the market or to change. Working cultures need to undergo mandatory changes, leadership must be exemplified in a different way and employees have long since ceased to be petitioners. But I also know from my many interviews with candidates as well as companies that the topic of comprehensiveness is a compelling one.

Only very few companies are ready to face these big transformation processes and, above all, forget one thing: With **digital transformation**, virtually everything is changing at a roaring speed. It is not only about IT processes. It concerns morals, philosophy, humanity in the best of senses, value change. This asks too much of management, employees, whole organizations - irrespective of a given industry.

Digital transformation expressly demands personal transformation. **To become digital means to be even more human.**

I've been busying myself intensely with social topics ever since my youth, both the ethical as well as the moral/philosophical backgrounds. Besides raising two wonderful daughters, who are now grown up and ready to plan and live their own lives, a fulfilled, uneven, but totally satisfying and instructive course of live up to now, with its heights and strokes of fate, which we all can't avoid, these topics have always been my driving force and still are today. I love humans and I enjoy interacting with them. My background with respect to my main job, as well as the additional training to become a hypnotherapist and coach (online and offline) , round up a holistic perspective and search for solutions both for individuals and companies.

- How do we manage to be content and yet to remain hungry for life?
- Are we really making an effort to understand other people, to understand ourselves?
- Do we pay close enough attention to ourselves?
- Do we have people looking after ourselves in case we can't cope so well?

- How do people cope with personal strokes of fate?
- How do our children feel when they see us constantly stressed out and strained?
- Are we role models?
- Can we serve as role models at all?
- Are we still able to trust?
- Ourselves, others?
- How frankly and openly do we deal with our intimate relationships?
- Do we know where our passions and talents are?
- Why are there so many people who, seemingly all of a sudden, get fears and phobias such as vertigo, fear of flying etc.?
- Why do you, for example, smoke or drink so much?
- Or why do you display an arrogant attitude in order to avoid emotional hurt?
- Why do you lie to the people who love you (children, family, partner) or who are financially dependent on you (employees), just to keep up appearances or to avoid conflict / the truth?

All of this concerns us first of all personally on the one hand, but it also reflects, of course, to our surroundings on the other hand, be it professionally or privately.

www.ingramcontent.com/pod-product-compliance
Lightning Source LLC
Chambersburg PA
CBHW070656220526
45466CB00001B/464